MW00780626

HowExpert Presents

How To Draw Animals

Your Step By Step Guide
To Drawing Animals

HowExpert with
Therese Barleta

For more tips related to this topic, visit
HowExpert.com/drawanimals.

Recommended Resources

- HowExpert.com – Quick 'How To' Guides on All Topics from A to Z by Everyday Experts.
- HowExpert.com/free – Free HowExpert Email Newsletter.
- HowExpert.com/books – HowExpert Books
- HowExpert.com/courses – HowExpert Courses
- HowExpert.com/clothing – HowExpert Clothing
- HowExpert.com/membership – HowExpert Membership Site
- HowExpert.com/affiliates – HowExpert Affiliate Program
- HowExpert.com/jobs – HowExpert Jobs
- HowExpert.com/writers – Write About Your #1 Passion/Knowledge/Expertise & Become a HowExpert Author.
- HowExpert.com/resources – Additional HowExpert Recommended Resources
- YouTube.com/HowExpert – Subscribe to HowExpert YouTube.
- Instagram.com/HowExpert – Follow HowExpert on Instagram.
- Facebook.com/HowExpert – Follow HowExpert on Facebook.
- TikTok.com/@HowExpert – Follow HowExpert on TikTok.

Publisher's Foreword

Dear HowExpert Reader,

HowExpert publishes quick 'how to' guides on all topics from A to Z by everyday experts.

At HowExpert, our mission is to discover, empower, and maximize everyday people's talents to ultimately make a positive impact in the world for all topics from A to Z...one everyday expert at a time!

All of our HowExpert guides are written by everyday people just like you and me, who have a passion, knowledge, and expertise for a specific topic.

We take great pride in selecting everyday experts who have a passion, real-life experience in a topic, and excellent writing skills to teach you about the topic you are also passionate about and eager to learn.

We hope you get a lot of value from our HowExpert guides, and it can make a positive impact on your life in some way. All of our readers, including you, help us continue living our mission of positively impacting the world for all spheres of influences from A to Z.

If you enjoyed one of our HowExpert guides, then please take a moment to send us your feedback from wherever you got this book.

Thank you, and we wish you all the best in all aspects of life.

Sincerely,

BJ Min
Founder & Publisher of HowExpert
HowExpert.com

PS...If you are also interested in becoming a HowExpert author, then please visit our website at HowExpert.com/writers. Thank you & again, all the best!

Table of Contents

Introduction

Have you been trying to draw animals? It can be hard, but using my drawings, I will teach you in this step-by-step guide how to animals.

I have been drawing as a job for a total of 5 years, but I have been practicing from what I see around me for around twenty years.

Even though I have been drawing that long, I still constantly practice and continuously learn. I encourage everyone who will read this guide to practice drawing and sketching everyday as well. Because this guide is about drawing animals, you must constantly observe animal structure and behavior in order to master how to draw particular animal.

With each day that you observe, sketch and practice sketching them, you will come one step closer to making your drawings more and more realistic.

Drawing Animals the Easy Way

Drawing animals is actually easier than most people make it out to be. It only looks intimidating at first, but once you discover the trick to mastering how to draw certain kinds of animals, the rest will come easily.

The keys to a successful drawing of an animal lie in:

- **Structure:** Each group of animals has a specific way that it's body is built. For example, dogs and wolves have more or less the same body structure. Another example are cats and wild animals, like the tiger. The size varies greatly, but the same structure of a cat's body can be found in a tiger's.
- **Movement:** This is especially important in active animals, such as dogs, cats and horses.
- **Texture:** Texture is important because this is how you can express in a drawing how a real animal's hide is supposed to be. The softness of a rabbit's fur, obviously, is different from the coarse hide of a rhinoceros.

Drawing Materials Explained

For drawing animals, you can use everything from a ballpoint pen to a brush and watercolor palette. But, since this is a learning guide, we'll just start with a pencil. With a pencil, you can always erase any mistake you have made, making it the ideal drawing tool to use.

For the drawings on this guide, I used the following:

- Blue pencil (for drafting and plotting).
- 7B pencil (for final drawing).
- 4B (for shading).
- Bond Paper/Copy Paper.

Setting up a 'Workshop'

Before actually sitting down to draw, you need to find a good spot where you can do so.

Finding a comfortable place is important because drawing takes a lot of time and you don't want to be in an uncomfortable place for long.

Find a table with a nice height—not too high or too low. A high table will just make your arm easily tired and throw your drawing proportions off, whereas a table that is too low will hurt your back and give you a headache from looking down too much.

Find a spot with good lighting. Bad lighting or places that are dim will just make your eyes tired and strained so, find a bright place to draw. Good lighting condition is also needed so you can see whether your drawing is correct, the shading is enough, etc.

Quick Tips: If you feel some discomfort in your wrist or hands:

- Take a pause from drawing, especially if you have been continuously drawing for more than an hour.
- Loosen up your hand/wrist/fingers by shaking them.
- Give your hand some stretching by closing your hands into a loose fist and then opening them, closing and then opening them again, gently.

- Stand up and do some arm stretching, especially if it is your whole arm that feels tense.

Chapter 1: Structure

The best practice for drawing animals is to study how they are shaped, structured, and how they move. Thankfully, domesticated animals are easy to observe, especially if you have your own pet at home. In the cases of wild animals, you can either go to the zoo or observe them using photos and videos.

Drawing materials used:

- Eraser.
- Blue pencil (drafting).
- 7B for the heavier lines.
- Triangle ruler (if you do not have this, any ruler will do).

Tips and pointers

Practice sketching in general shapes. It doesn't have to be a fully detailed drawing in one sitting. Just a loose sketch every now, and then during the day helps sharpens your skills in capturing the general size and shape of your animal subject.

Step-by-step instructions on getting the structure

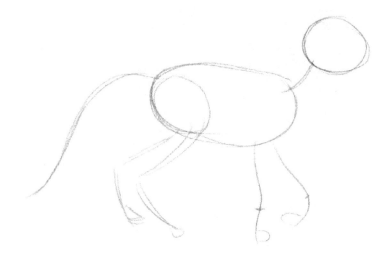

Figure 1. Preliminary sketch of a cat's wireframes.

Figure 2. Wireframes with added details

1. Start out first by drawing lines or 'frameworks'.

Figure 3. Wireframe that has been fleshed-out

2. Slowly fill-in the framework with 'bulk' by sketching out the general shape of the animal.

Figure 4. Drawing of a cat with shading and details

3. Erase some of the lines as you start to add more detail to the drawing.

Chapter 2: Movement

A large part of giving life to drawing animals is by capturing how a particular animal moves. This is especially important when drawing horses, which have a specific way of moving and are often drawn while running.

Drawing materials used:

- 7B for outlining.
- 4B for shading.
- Eraser.

Tips and pointers

Again, observing how a particular animal moves will help you a lot in capturing animal movement. Looking at photos and videos of animals in movement is a good way to study them.

Step-by-step instructions on how to draw animal movement

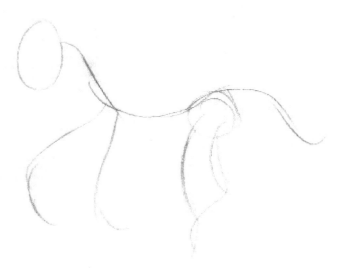

Figure 5. Sketch the wireframe of the movement

Figure 6. Wireframe with more details in it

1. Make a basic outline or a wireframe of the
    animal's movement. It should just be the
    general direction of movement that the animal
    is taking.

Figure 7. Wireframe with more 'bulk' in it

2. Now, start to give the wireframe some bulk by adding the general shapes that that particular animal has.

Figure 8. Wireframes with erased lines

3. Erase some of the lines so that you have a cleaner outline.

Figure 9. Final drawing with details and shading

4. Proceed in adding more details to your
    drawing. Put some motion lines and dirt flying
    to make the horse appear more like it's moving.
    Notice that there is also movement in the hair
    and tail.

Chapter 3: Texture and Basic Shading

Different animals have different kinds of fur or skin texture. Being able to show that in your drawing is part of achieving a successful animal drawing. You do not draw a rabbit's fur the same as a rhinoceros' hide. Even in more similar comparisons, like with cats and dogs, a cat's fur is different in texture different than a dog's, even if they both have fur. This is why it is important to study how different animal coats, hide, and furs look like, and how to be able to draw them accurately.

Drawing materials used:

- 7B for outlining.
- 4B for shading.
- Eraser.

Tips and pointers

The secret lies in the pencil stroke weight, direction, and length. For example, a golden retriever's fur is created with longer, flatter strokes than a short-haired cat, and a horse's hide is generally drawn in smooth strokes and not stipples, like when drawing fine fur. How you hold the pencil can help. When creating broader, smoother strokes, holding your pencil at a low angle (resulting in the duller end of the pencil landing against the paper) helps. Lightly holding the pencil on its sharp end helps in creating fine lines and stippling can help create the illusion of grainy-ness of roughness.

Step-by-Step instructions on how to draw animal hide texture

Figure 10. Example of a dog's wireframe

1. The first thing in drawing an animal is always the wireframes. Adding texture is more on the detail part so, first we must make the wireframes.

Figure 11. General shapes comprise of basic shapes such as circles triangles, cones etc.

2. As you have previously learned, add dimension to the drawing by sketching out the animal's general shape. Next, add the details. This is where drawing the fur comes in. Depending on the type of animal, you will have to draw the fur in a particular way.

Figure 12. An example of soft small pencil strokes for the fur

3. For soft furred-animals, draw with thin lines to express softness and suppleness of the fur.

Figure 13. a dog has longer and thicker fur than a rabbit

4. For animals with longer and thicker fur, make your pencil strokes longer and 'flatter'.

Figure 14. notice the 'sheen' of the skin of the horse

5. For animals with smooth hides, like the horse, expressing sheen makes the drawing look effective. Evenly shading the animal subject helps in expressing this kind of texture.

Figure 15. Dotting and shading help bring out the rough texture of the iguana's skin

6. For animals with coarse hides like iguanas, make sure to show the rough texture of the skin by adding lots of wrinkling lines.

Figure 16. Notice the shininess and slipperiness of the skin of the snake

7. Some animals have shiny, slippery skin, like the snake and to express this on paper, you must make the skin look as glossy as possible by highlighting and shading strongly.

Chapter 4: How to Draw Cats

There are different breeds of cat. In this tutorial, we will focus mainly on the short-haired common house cat to better illustrate how the cat's body is shaped without the thick fur.

Drawing materials used:

- 7B for outlining
- 4B for shading
- Eraser

Tips and pointers

In learning how to draw a cat, make sure to pay close attention to how the head is shaped, the fur quality, and the way the legs are drawn. Although there are different breeds of cats, the common short-haired house cat looks less bulky than the Persian kind, and the face is 'fuller' with the area of the nose being more elevated than the Persian type.

While drawing cats, keep in mind that cats are usually soft bodied, light, graceful animals so, try to convey those things in your drawing. The cat often has a stoic and snobbish look on its face when it is not curious. The cat's fur is soft and thin compared to dogs, and it's good to take note of that when drawing cats.

Step-by-step instructions on how to draw a cat

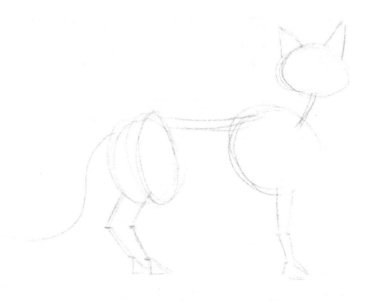

Figure 17. Wireframe of a cat

1. As you learned in the previous chapters, drawing an animal begins with making the wireframe. Cats will generally have a wireframe that looks like the picture above.

Figure 18. Wireframe modified into cylinders

2. Now that you have a guide for estimating
    where the features will lie, you can start adding
    to them by bulking up the wire-frame with
    basic shapes of circles and cylinders. The joints
    of the limbs are represented by small circles.

Figure 19. Erase some of the lines to achieve a cleaner outline

3. At this point, you'll be able to outline the body of the cat. It is easier to start with the main outline first before adding in the details. Feel free to erase the wireframe and the bulked wire-frame guide so you have a cleaner looking drawing.

Figure 20. The outline as fur in short, thin strokes

4. In drawing cats, rather than drawing a flat continuous line, it is better to draw the outline as fur in short thin strokes.

Figure 21. Draw the cat's eyes as wide but almond shaped

5. Now that you have an outline for the body, you can add the details starting with the face. You can start with the eyes. Drawing the cat's eyes

is important as this is one of its prominent features. The cat's eyes are almond shape (although when alert, the eyes tend to look rounder and bigger, but, still slanted and pointed at the ends).

Figure 22. The cat's nose's general shape is an inverted triangle

6. The cat's nose is small and inverted-triangle shaped so, start with an inverted triangle before adding in the small nostrils.

Figure 23. The mouth as an inverted 'Y' shape

7. Draw the mouth by making two lines starting from the base of the nose outward. Add dots around the mouth and add the whiskers by drawing thin lines outwards. Make sure the

lines are not heavy and it should taper from heavy to thin, like so:

Figure 24. Start shading delicately on the face

8. Make some shading to bring out the solidity of the cat's face. Shade delicately and shade by using soft kinds of pencil strokes. These kinds of strokes can be achieved by tilting your pencil and using the flatter end so the shading comes out broad, but smooth.

Figure 25. start shading the body and adding markings and details

9. Add more volume by adding additional details of fur on the body. Some cats have markings on the face and tail. In this example, the cat has them all over his body.

Figure 26. Finalized drawing of a cat

10. Finalize the drawing by adding more shading
    that will help bring out the general shape of the
    cat.

Chapter 5: How to Draw Dogs

In this chapter, we are going to learn how to draw dogs, particularly the Golden Retriever breed so as not to confuse with the wolf in the later parts of this book. Dogs and wolves are similar, but you will soon learn some notable differences between the two.

Drawing materials used:

- 7B for outlining.
- 4B for shading.
- Eraser.

Tips and pointers

In learning how to draw a dog, it is important to pay close attention to how the head is shaped, the fur quality, and the way the legs are drawn. Dogs usually have a head that plateaus at the top and their snouts are quite long and prominent, making the mouth wide and the nose is larger than a cat's. When the mouth is open, some teeth are shown.

As opposed to cats, dogs are usually larger, more 'rough-bodied', more muscular, and bulky as well. Their fur is significantly coarser than that of the cat and has a sheen that the soft, matte-looking fur of a cat does not. The dog usually has a warm and friendly look on its face (given it's not angry, of course) so, try to bring all of these elements into your drawing when drawing a dog.

Step-by-step instructions on how to draw a dog

Figure 27. Wireframe for drawing a dog

1. As with drawing a cat, drawing a dog also begins with making the wireframe. Dogs

41

usually have a wireframe that looks like the picture above when standing.

Figure 28. Wireframe converted into more general shapes

2. Now that you have a guide for estimating where the features will lie, you can start adding them by filling up the wire-frame with basic shapes of circles and cylinders. The joints of the limbs are represented by small circles. The torso area of the dog is quite bigger than the rear end of it, as you can see in this example so, try to pattern your drawing after that.

Figure 29. Create the basic outline

3. At this point you'll be able to outline the body of the dog. It is easier to start with the main outline first before adding in the details. Feel free to erase the wireframe and the bulked wire-frame guide so you have a cleaner looking drawing.

Figure 30. Draw the final outline as thin short strokes

4. Like in drawing cats, it is better to draw the fur as the outline itself rather than drawing a flat, continuous line. The fur should be illustrated in feathered strokes, like above.

Figure 31. Make the dog's eyes look friendly

5. Now that you have an outline for the body, you can add the details starting with the face. You can start with the eyes. Drawing the dog's eyes in a way that it conveys friendliness is important as this is one of its prominent features. The dog's eyes are usually rounder than a cat's.

Figure 32. The dog's nose is rounder compared to cats

6. The dogs' nose is also a kind of inverted-triangle, but it is of a softer and rounder variety. You can start with an inverted triangle with rounded edges before adding in the nostrils.

Figure 33. The dog's mouth

7. Draw the mouth by making two lines starting from the base of the nose outward and a bit turned down at the ends. In this drawing, the dog's mouth is open and the tongue hangs out—something that the dog commonly does so, we're going to draw the mouth like this in this guide. Add dots around the nose and add the whiskers by drawing thin lines outwards. Make sure the lines are not heavy and it should taper from heavy to thin, like above.

Figure 34. Start shading the dog's face

8. Make some shading to bring out the solidity of the dog's face. Shade delicately and shade by using these kinds of pencil strokes (see below). These kinds of strokes can be achieved by tilting your pencil and using the flatter end so the shading comes out broad, but smooth.

Figure 35. Drawing of a dog with added details

9. Add more volume by adding additional details
   of fur on the body but putting more feathered
   strokes like in making the outline of its body.

Figure 36. Final drawing, complete with shading

10. Make sure to make the body look like it has
    more dimension and volume by adding more
    shading to the legs and near the neck.

Chapter 6: How to Draw a Bear

In this chapter, we will be tackling on the topic of how to draw bears. As with dogs and cats there are also different types of bears but the one we will discuss here is how to draw the brown bear, otherwise known as the grizzly bear. Once you learn how to draw the brown bear, you will have what you need for the foundations of drawing any kind of bear. Let's begin.

Drawing materials used:

- 7B for outlining.
- 4B for shading.
- Eraser.

Tips and pointers

In learning how to draw a bear, it is important to pay close attention to how the head is shaped, the fur quality, and the way the body is drawn. Bears tend to have big heads and long, thick neck covered with coarse hair (like the rest of their body) and their muzzle is big and strong. They have big scary teeth when their mouths are open, however we will focus more on the body shape of the bear in this chapter. Another thing of note is its big bulky body and the huge paws that are flat and long compared to other animals that have paws. The ears of the bear however

are round, rather small, and not pointed like some
animals.

Step-by-step instructions on how to draw a bear

Figure 37. Wireframe for drawing a bear

1. You can begin by drawing the wireframe of the
   bear's body when drawing a bear. Start with a
   circle for the head and a cone cut off at the tip
   for the muzzle. A big oval shape can represent
   the shoulder-torso area, then connect the head
   to that area with a line.

Figure 38. Wireframe with added 'bulk'

2. Now that you have a guide for estimating
    where the parts of the body lie, it's time to fill-
    up the wire-frame lines with more solid shapes,
    like circles and cylinders. As usual, the joints of
    the limbs are represented by small circles. The
    torso area of a bear, like the dog is quite bigger
    than the rear end of it. The line that connects
    the shoulder/torso area can now be connected
    to the rear by drawing like above.

Figure 39. Erase unneeded lines

3. At this point, you'll be able to make the outline for the body of a bear. Feel free to erase the wireframes and other un-needed lines for a cleaner looking drawing. After that, add the outline as short strokes that represent fur as outlining thickly will just make it look two-dimensional.

Figure 40. Bears have dark eyes that are relatively small

4. Now that you have an outline for the body, you can add the details starting with the face. You can start with the eyes then add the nose. Bears have dark eyes that are relatively small compared to its face.

Figure 41. the muzzle is big and the nose is rounded

5. The nose of the bear is round and big compared to, say, the dog or the cat. So, draw it big at the tip of the muzzle and shade it dark.

Figure 42. the mouth curves outward

6. Draw the mouth by making two lines starting from the base of the nose outward and then curving up near the nose.

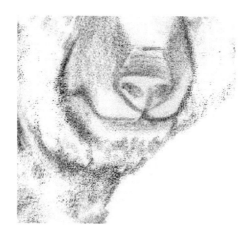

Figure 43. Shade around the muzzle

7. Make some shading to bring out the shape of the bear's muzzle. The bear we drew is facing front so it's length is foreshortened. Because of that, we have to compensate with shading. The shading must still make the muzzle look long. Shade delicately by the sides of the nose and mouth and shade by using these kinds of pencil strokes (see below.) These kinds of strokes can be achieved by tilting your pencil and using the flatter end so the shading comes out broad, but smooth.

Figure 44. Shade around the eyes

8. Bring some depth to the face around the eyes by making short strokes that look like fur.

Figure 45. finished drawing of a bear

9. Put details on the body by shading in short stippled strokes.

Chapter 7: How to Draw Lion

In this chapter, we will be tackling on the topic of how to draw lions. All lions look relatively the same (except some are somewhat bigger, some are skinnier). The female looks different from the male in that it has no thick coat of hair/fur on its head-neck area. Our main point of focus in this chapter is drawing the male lion.

Drawing materials used:

- 7B for outlining.
- 4B for shading.
- Eraser.

Tips and pointers

In learning how to draw a lion, it is important to pay close attention to how the head is shaped, the texture of the fur, and the way the body is drawn. You will notice that in drawing a lion, the head seems to be the biggest part and then it tapers (becomes narrower) towards the rear. This is due to the fact that the lion's head is hairy and the volume of the lion's hair adds to the bulk of it. We need to look past that volume of hair first if we are to draw the lion properly.

Step-by-step instructions on how to draw a lion

Figure 46. Lion wireframe

1. Let's begin by drawing the wireframe of the lion's using a medium sized circle for the head, a big circle for the shoulder to torso area, and then another medium sized circle for the rear. At this point you can have small circles to represent the part where the shoulder and leg joints are.

Figure 47. Add the muzzle

2. Add the muzzle to the circle (representing the head by drawing a cylinder) .

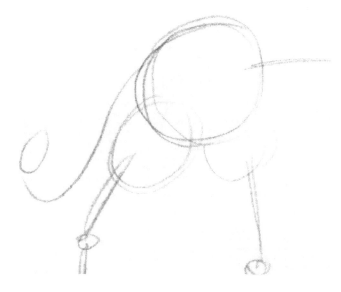

Figure 48. Use fluid lines like the lines used in making the lion's tail

3. The wireframe should look something like the cats', only bigger. Try not to make the wireframe look stiff, as following a stiff wireframe can result in a stiff looking drawing. Use flowing, fluid pencil strokes.

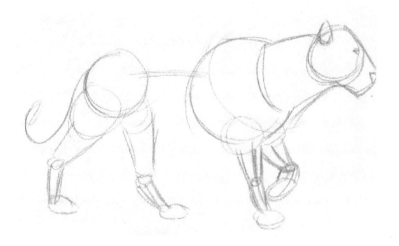

Figure 49. Wireframe for the lion's body

4. After finishing the wireframe, you can now bulk-up your drawing using the general shapes we have been using in the previous chapters. Cylinders are great for fleshing out the legs and circles are a great way to pinpoint where the joints bend. Connect the shoulder area with the rear area such that it tapers toward the rear. Draw the neck thickly.

Figure 50. the muzzle of a lion is shorter but thicker.

5. Compared to the bear, the muzzle of the lion is shorter and wider, so, draw it like the above drawing.

6. Add the details of the face by drawing the ears, the eyes and the nose. Put dots just below the nose and add whiskers by drawing with thin lines.

Figure 51. Make the hair look bushy

7. Now comes the part where we add the hair to the head-neck portion of the lion. Begin by outlining the fur around a centimeter away from the neck of the lion. Erase the neck-outline then proceed on making strokes of the lion's fur around the neck. The fur around that area should look thick and bushy.

Figure 52.Begin shading the body

8. Shade the body of the lion by making broad
    smooth strokes. The lion has very short fur
    around the body so, there is not much need to
    detail strokes of it. Broad strokes of shading
    will do.

Figure 53. Add the details of the face

9. Bring some depth to the face by the making light shading around it.

Figure 54. finalized drawing of a lion

10. Finalize the drawing by adding more shading to bring out the shape of the body.

Chapter 8: How to Draw a Bird

In this chapter, we take on how to draw Birds. There are a lot of species of birds, more than you can counts with your fingers. Unfortunately, we cannot exhaust how to draw each and every one of them in this chapter so, for now, we will just concentrate on one kind, a small type of bird.

Drawing materials used:

- 7B for outlining.
- 4B for shading.
- Eraser.

Tips and pointers

Drawing the feathers is the most important thing to learn when drawing birds. In drawing this type of bird, pay attention to how the beak is shaped, and how big the head is in proportion to the body, as well as how the legs are shaped. The bird's legs are very much unlike the legs of the previous animals we have tackled. The bird's legs are twiggy and do not have the same bulk as the cat or the dog, although larger birds do have thicker legs. You'll notice that the body of the bird we are going to draw is roundish so the wire-frame won't be difficult to create. Let's begin.

Step-by-step instructions on how to draw a bird

Figure 55. bird wireframe

1. For this type of bird, the wireframe will just consist of two circles, one big (for the body) the smaller one for the head, and then two lines for the legs then crescent shaped lines for the feet and then a rectangular shape for the tail.

Figure 56. Wireframe with the wings attached closely

2. Add the basic strokes for the 'folded wings' to the body and the beak. Imagine the wings folded closely to the body such that it is tightly wrapped on its back.

Figure 57. Cleaner outline

3. At this point, you'll be able to make the outline for the body of the bird. Feel free to erase the wireframes particularly at the neck a cleaner looking drawing. After that, draw the feathers in longs strokes one on top of the other the image above.

Figure 58. Notice the shiny and bead-like eyes

4. Now that you have an outline for the body, you can add the details of the face. You can start with the eyes. The bird's eyes are beady and round so, make it look round and shiny.

Figure 59. the wings are folded on top of one another

5. When drawing the wings, as mentioned earlier, imagine it folded on top of the other since the bird we are drawing is perched and not in flight. Draw the feathers of the wings and make them look layered on top of one another, the first layer on the top is shorter and the second layer is longer.

Figure 60. shade to make the wings look glossy

6. At this point, you will have to rely heavily on
    shading. Try to make the head and the body of
    the bird look round and plump by shading in
    soft strokes from dark to light as if you were
    shading a ball. Make broad soft shading on the
    beak.

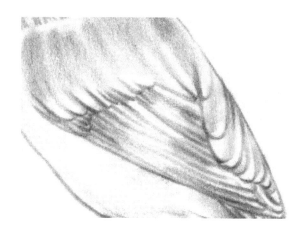

Figure 61. Use fine, broad strokes

7. Shade the wings by putting long broad, but soft strokes of the pencil inside the feathers you outlined.

Figure 62. Shade the legs and claw

8. Next shade the legs and claws also using broad long, but light pencil strokes.

Figure 63. Final drawing of a bird

9. Shade more darkly to bring out the shape of the bird's body.

Chapter 9: How to Draw a Horse

In this chapter, you will learn how to draw horses. Like other animals, there are several types of horses. There are types that are short and rather stocky, there are types that have hair near the hooves, there are types whose legs are thicker, but the one we will learn to draw here is the more common type of horse.

Drawing materials used:

- 7B for outlining
- 4B for shading
- Eraser

Tips and pointers

The horse is one of the most popular animal subjects to draw for because it unites strength and grace. The horse is a muscular animal so, when drawing horses, shading will be one of the things you will have to pay attention to. At the same time, you must be careful not to draw it stiffly. The horse is a creature of movement so that must be apparent in your drawing. It looks best when it is moving, but for this chapter, we will focus on how to draw the parts of it so you can draw it in motion the next time. Knowing the main parts of the horse and how to shade it comes very much in handy in how to bring alive a drawing of a horse. Let's begin.

Step-by-Step Instructions on how to draw a horse

Figure 64. Wireframe of the horse

1. First, draw the wireframes by making two circles on slightly larger than the other. Then make another circle to represent the head and attach a cone to it as the muzzle. Connect the circles with lines then proceed to making the wireframe of the tail, the legs, the hooves, and the joints as follows.

Figure 65. Convert the wireframe into cylindrical shapes

2. Next fill-out the wireframes by thickening the parts into general shapes using cylindrical or tube-like shapes. The legs should be thickened out into conical shapes that taper or become narrower as they reach the hooves. The neck should look like a thick cone connected to the head. Add some ears to the head.

Figure 66. Erase unneeded lines for a cleaner outline

3. You can now begin to make a clean outline by
    erasing the extra lines when you made the
    wireframe. Draw the outline using smoother
    and more curved lines. You can also now add a
    rough sketch of the hair and tail.

Figure 67. Cleaner and more detailed outline of the horse

4. Now that you have an outline for the body, you can add the details of the face. You can start with the eyes by drawing a circle and then an arc over it. The nose can be drawn as a nostril and the mouth as a line under it.

Figure 68. Preliminary shading on the outline

5. Now comes the shading. This part is a bit tricky
    and you'll need to look at various pictures of
    horses to get a feel of where to shade. Basically,
    you have to make the horse look muscular and
    that can be illustrated by shading in the right
    places by the legs and the shoulder area, as well
    as the neck. Horses use their shoulders and
    legs a lot in running so, this is where the most
    muscles are.

Figure 69. Left light shading, right: shading built up to look darker

6. When shading the horses' body, you can start by making light strokes then build up heavier shading by focusing on the parts that should look 'deeper'. Use broad and smooth pencil strokes when shading so it looks more realistic. Be sure to make the transition from heavier to light shading by shading smoothly.

Figure 70. Draw the hair in smooth strokes

7. Draw the hair and tail in smooth flowing strokes to convey movement.

Figure 71. Finished drawing of a horse

8. Shade the legs and face similarly as you would shade the body.

Chapter 10: How to Draw an Elephant

In this chapter, you will learn how to draw elephants. There are two types of elephants: The African and the Asian variety. The Asian elephant is smaller in size with smaller ears, but a big domed head relative to its body and the African variety is bigger in size with bigger ears and larger tusks. The type of elephant we will learn in this chapter is the African elephant.

Drawing materials used:

- 7B for outlining.
- 4B for shading.
- Eraser.

Tips and pointers

The elephant is quite an interesting animal to draw. Its features are very unique from other animals and you can tell straight away from an outline that a creature is an elephant. It is a large creature with big ears, a long trunk, and long tusks with a hunching back and wrinkly skin. In drawing elephants, we must try to bring out these characteristics, especially the bulkiness of this animal and the wrinkly texture of its hide and the movement of its trunk. Let's begin.

Step-by-step instructions on how to an elephant

Figure 72. Start the wireframe of the elephant by making three large circles and flowing lines for the tail and trunk

1. The wireframe of an elephant can be drawn beginning with three circles, two large circles of relatively the same size next to each other. Then make another circle to represent the head and attach a flowing line to represent the trunk and then large triangular shapes for the ear.

Figure 73. Add the wireframe of the legs

2. Next, make straight lines with small circles as joints to represent the legs, and then some lines to represent the tail.

Figure 74. Thickened outline

3. Next, erase the inner parts of the wireframes and connect the outer lines of the circles more. The legs should be thickened out significantly into conical shapes. The elephant's legs should be large tube-like shapes which ends in three nail-like attachments at the bottom. The neck is almost invisible due to the size of the head and the close attachment of it to the body, however, you need to create some sagging skin by the neck area and then add the ears.

Figure 75. Outline of the elephant

4. Now that you have an outline for the body, refine the drawing of the head by thickening out the line that represents the trunk. Draw it such that it narrows towards the end of the line. After that you can start adding the details of the face. Add the eyes by drawing a circle and then an arc over it. Shade the circle darkly, add the details of the mouth by adding a small lip under the trunk and making a line curving upwards.

Figure 76. be sure to capture the wrinkly texture of the skin

5. Now comes the shading and detailing. You can start adding the 'wrinkles' by drawing crisscross lines across the skin. Try not to make it look like stiff, and even grill-like lines. The wrinkles should be more prominent around areas that should be darkly shaded.

Figure 77. Use broad strokes

6. You can make broader pencil strokes by the legs, under the ears and chin, at the belly, and by the head after that.

Figure 78. Add the details on the trunk

7. Draw the tail in strokes going downward and add some wrinkle lines on the trunk as well.

Figure 79. finalized drawing of the elephant

8. Add the tusks by drawing crescent lines and then shade under it.

Chapter 11: How to Draw a Penguin

Like the other animals there are also different kinds of penguins. In this chapter, we will focus on the more recognizable type of the bunch, the King Penguin. This type is bigger than the other types and the most commonly drawn type when people draw penguins.

Drawing materials used:

- 7B for outlining.
- 4B for shading.
- Eraser.

Tips and pointers

Like the elephant, the penguin is also quite easy to recognize because of its unique posture and the way the body is built compared to other birds. You'll notice that the penguin looks like it's 'standing up' vertically like a human would. Its wings are also one of its more unique features as it looks like a dolphin's or a shark's fin rather than wings with feathers like other birds. Its legs are short and stocky compared to its relative height, something that causes it to wobble when walking. Let's get more into the details as we begin the drawing instructions for how to draw a penguin.

Step-by-step instructions on how to a penguin

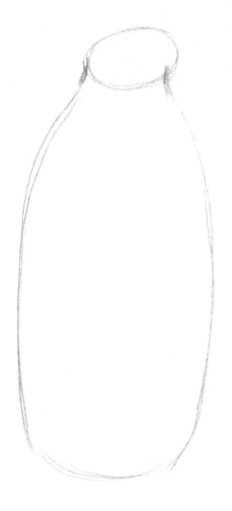

Figure 80.The penguin's wireframe looks like a bottle

1. When making the wire-frame for the penguin, think of a bottle with a very short neck, or a bottle's 'body' with no neck and a ball attached to it's top—that is more or less how one would construct a penguin's wire frame. There won't be much need for thickening out the basic structure after that.

Figure 81. Cone-like shapes for the feet

2. Next, add cone-like shapes for the legs and elongated oval shapes for the feet.

Figure 82. Draw the head shaped like an egg

3. Add the beak and make a small circle to indicate the eyes.

Figure 83. Create flowing lines with your pencil

4. Make two flowing lines for the wings.

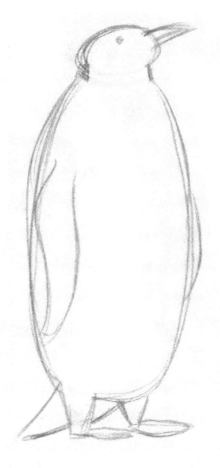

Figure 84. Bulked outline of a penguin

5. Now that you have the general shape ready, you can erase the extra, unneeded lines and continue on to smoothing out the outline of your drawing.

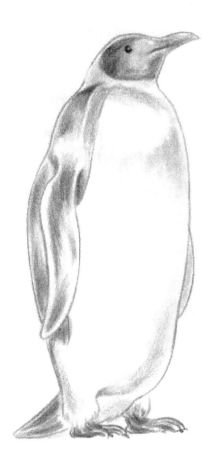

Figure 85. Begin shading the penguin's body

6. After outlining the drawing comes the shading.
   Another unique thing about the penguin, is the
   markings of it. The king penguin's markings
   consist of a white belly, yellow markings near
   the neck (we are just drawing with a pencil so
   that won't show) a black colored face and back,
   all up to the tail. The legs are white, but the feet
   are black. With that knowledge, we can begin

shading the penguin. Begin shading the parts
that are black darkly.

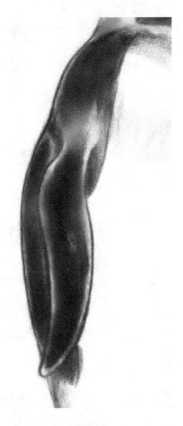

Figure 86. Darken your shading

7. Put highlights on certain parts, like the wings
   and near the face, at the back, at the toes to
   make it look realistic.

Figure 87. Highlighting makes the shape standout

8. Shade the parts that are supposed to be white delicately. Just shade lightly near the top of the chest and the bottom between the legs, the leg area, and the 'lower stomach area.' Use broad and smooth pencil strokes when shading the white parts.

Figure 88. Notice how the beak and eyes are shaded

9. Draw the details of the face which is the slit at the mouth and the beady looking eyes. To draw

the mouth, you just have to create a flowing line between the beak and to draw the eyes, make a small circle, and shade it darkly leaving just a spot of white as the eye-highlight.

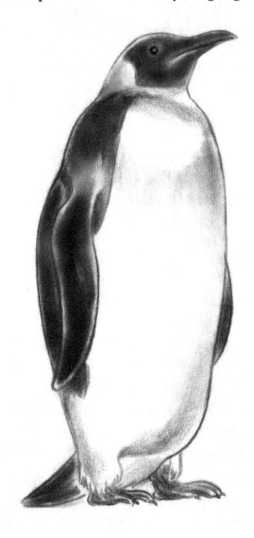

Figure 89. Final drawing of the penguin

Chapter 12: How to Draw a Hamster

Hamsters are fairly easy to draw once you observe them enough. These creatures are quite similar to other rodents so, the body structure is more or less the same. If you have a pet hamster, it will be easier for you to draw a hamster since you are already familiar with how it looks without need—or with less need for a picture or video reference.

Drawing materials used:

- 7B for outlining.
- 4B for shading.
- Eraser.

Tips and pointers

As I have said earlier, the hamster's body is similar to other rodents. One of the main differences is the fur quality of the hamster. The hamster has thick, long, and soft hair, but underneath all the hair, its body is quite long and tubular. For this chapter, we will focus on the general shape of it and how to illustrate the hamster's fluffiness. Be sure to pay attention to capturing that particular quality, as it is the most defining characteristic of the hamster. Let's begin.

Step-by-step instructions on how to a hamster

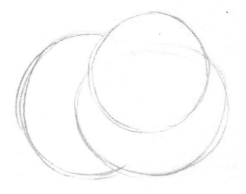

Figure 90. Start by drawing 3 circles

1. You can start drawing a hamster by making three circles. In this pose that we are going to do, the body of the hamster is foreshortened so the face and the front part of the body is more visible than the back or the middle part. That being said, draw the circles one on top of the other like above and the ear.

Figure 91. Draw circles for the snout

2. Draw a smaller circle for the snout and some arcs around the circle representing the face as the cheeks. Draw the eyes, the nose, and mouth tentatively. The noses' general shape is an inverted triangle while the mouth is an inverted 'Y' shape.

Figure 92. Draw triangles as feet

3. Draw straight lines for the legs and then small triangular shapes for the feet.

Figure 93. The legs are thickened into cone-like shapes

4. At this point you can start thickening the legs into inverted cone-like shapes and then erase some of the unneeded lines around the body, particularly where the front part of the body is adjacent to the legs and the middle lines between the front and rear.

Figure 94. Bring out the fluffiness in your strokes when drawing the fur

5. After outlining the drawing, change the outline into feathered strokes that represent hair/fur. For a hairy, furry animal, like the hamster, it is better to outline it with pencil strokes that look like hair as opposed to a stiff flat line that will not convey the soft texture that the fur should possess.

Figure 95. Add some shading

6. Add broad and smooth pencil strokes to add depth to the shape of the hamster. Shade delicately around the underside part of the hamster and the legs. Shading at the middle will also help make it look fuller.

Figure 96. Draw the fingers with 'u' like shapes

7. Add further details by making more feathered pencil strokes by the underside and the middle.

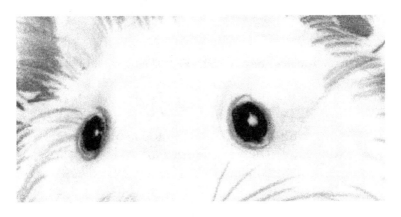

Figure 97. Make the eyes look beady

8. Draw the details of the face hamster by darkening the circles of its eyes. A hamster's eyes should look beady and shiny so make it appear that way by shading it darkly and evenly.

Figure 98. the nose and mouth can be brought out by shading

9. Erase the line at the top of the nose. Make it look less triangular by softening the edges into more rounded shapes. Shade around the nose delicately then shade the ears to look hollow. Add the whiskers by making long stokes outward with your pencil.

Figure 99. Finalized drawing of the hamster

10. Detail the hands by drawing small 'u' like shapes as the fingers, then put a small dash line as the nails.

Chapter 13: How to Draw a Zebra

The zebra is one of the zoo animals that have characteristics that make them easy to identify. They also have characteristics that are already quite familiar since they look similar to horses, ponies, and donkeys. With that in mind, in drawing zebras we must be careful to note their difference with these animals that they look similar to.

Drawing materials used:

- 7B for outlining.
- 4B for shading.
- Eraser.

Tips and pointers

As mentioned earlier, zebras are quite similar to horses and animals that look like horses. It is important to note, however, that there are differences between them that we must not confuse with one another. One of those differences is height and hair. The horse is typically larger than the zebra, the legs are longer, and the hair is different. The zebra's hair doesn't grow as long as the horse's and the tail is also different. The tail of the zebra only has hair near the tip, unlike the horse which has full flowing hair at the tail when grown out. And then, finally there is the most obvious difference that makes the zebra significantly unique: it's stripes.

Step-by-step instructions on how to a zebra

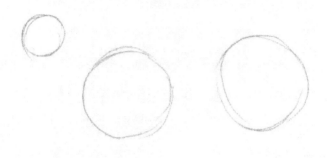

Figure 100. Start by drawing 3 circles

1. You can start drawing a zebra by making three circles. Two big ones roughly the size of each other (for the shoulder area and rear) and one small one to represent the head.

**Figure 101. A circle and a cone like shape makes a good
outline for the head**

2. Add a cone like shape that's cut off at the tip for
   the zebra's muzzle. Next, add small circles to
   represent the joints where the legs connect to
   the body. The rear circle should be bigger than
   the one in the front. Add straight lines to
   represent the legs and put small circle to
   represent the knees. Add small triangles to
   represent the hooves.

Figure 102. Draw the neck thickly

3. Now you can thicken-out the wireframes by connecting the shoulder part and the rear with two lines, and then joining the head with the shoulder by adding two lines again. After this, you should have something that looks like the neck and the body.

Figure 103. Draw parallel lines around the wireframe of the limbs

4. Draw the legs thicker around the wireframe.

Figure 104. add the wireframe for the hair

5. Add an outline of the hair and tail as well as the hooves, like above.

Figure 105. Cleaner zebra outline

6. Erase any unneeded lines like those at the neck, at the middle parts of the body that connects to the legs, and at the knees.
7. Smoothen out your lines.

Figure 106. outline with smoothened lines

8. After outlining the drawing, you can now detail it. With the zebra, you don't have to draw any fur as the skin of it is leathery. You can begin detailing by adding the eyes. The eyes are drawn by making an arc and a crescent next to each other and a circle inside it. Once you have made the circle, fill it out with dark shading, but leave a small circle inside it as the highlight. Add the nostril by making a dark circle near the end of the muzzle. It doesn't need to be a full circle just half will make it appear more real. Add a line for the mouth.

Figure 107. Lighter shading in the middle makes the image look more three-dimensional

9. This time we detail the whole body by adding its stripes. The zebra's stripes thicken along the middle part and get thinner around the face-part. To make it look more real, shade smoothly and darken around the tips of the stripes to make it look more 3-dimensional. Highlight along the middle of the stripes.

Figure 108. Added shading for the zebra's body

10. Add detail to the hair by making short strokes for the hair such that it looks a bit like a brush, and then draw the hair by the tail at the ends of it.

Figure 109. finalized drawing of the zebra

11. Add after that you can add the shading at the legs and the underside of the zebra as well as the face.

Chapter 14: How to Draw a Monkey

Drawing a monkey will be remarkably different from drawing any of the animals that we have studied so far. Drawing a monkey will be more similar to drawing a human than an animal due to its posture, its face structure, and the way the hands are shaped as well as the feet. Learning how to draw a monkey may be a challenge at first, but athe more you practice, the easier it will get.

Drawing materials used:

- 7B for outlining.
- 4B for shading.
- Eraser.

Tips and pointers

Do not be intimidated by the fact that drawing a monkey is similar to drawing a human. If anything, you will be able to understand better how it is drawn because the shape of the limbs, hands, and feet look familiar. In this chapter, we will tackle how to draw a monkey, a chimpanzee to be more correct. In actuality, the chimpanzee is an entirely different species from the monkey, it is an ape rather, but common knowledge often lumps the two together. We will not dig deep into that anymore, however. Let us focus on learning how to draw the chimpanzee.

Step-by-step instructions on how to a monkey

Figure 110. Draw three circles for the head, torso and rear

1. You can start drawing a chimp by making three circles. Three circles: One for the shoulder area, a smaller one for the rear, and an even smaller one to represent the head.

Figure 111. Add lines for the limbs

2. After drawing the circles, connect them together with a line. Next, add lines to represent the limbs and small circles to represent the joints where the legs connect to the body. Put small circle to represent the knees. Add small circles to represent the hands and feet.

Figure 112. Add triangle like shapes for the hands

3. Since the chimp's feet is shaped like our own feet, more or less, we need to draw it as a ball connected to a triangle by a line, like above.

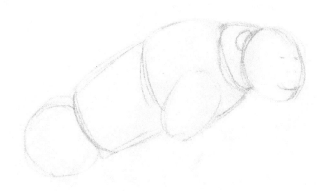

Figure 113. thickened outline of the monkey

4. Now you can thicken-out the wireframes by connecting the shoulder part and the rear with two lines, and then joining the head with the shoulder by adding two lines again. After this, you should have something that looks like the neck and the body. You should end up with a torso that looks like a wide tube.

Figure 114. imagining the limbs as tubes can help you visualize properly while drawing

5. Draw the legs and arms thicker around the wireframe. You should also end up with them looking like tubes connected together with circles as the joints.

Figure 115. The hands look like human hands, but with longer fingers

6. Add lines to represent fingers for the hands.

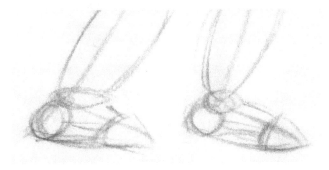

Figure 116. General shape of the monkey's foot

7. Make the feet appear more like feet by connecting the 'ball' with the triangle with two lines.

Figure 117. Erase the unnecessary lines

8. Erase any unneeded lines, like those at the
    neck, at the middle parts of the body that
    connects to the legs, and at the knees.
    Smoothen out your lines.

Figure 118. Begin drawing a fur outline

9. After outlining the drawing, you can now detail it. The chimpanzee is quite a hairy animal so, do not outline with a single line. Outline with flicks of your pencil to make it look like fur or hair like so.

Figure 119. Do not draw fur on the hands and feet

10. The whole body should be outlined with fur, except the palms and the underside of the feet.

Figure 120. Begin adding the details of the face

11. You can begin detailing further by adding the elements of the face. Draw the eyes much like a human's by drawing an arc and then a crescent on top of each other, and then add a circle in the middle. Once you have made the circle, fill it out with dark shading, but leave a small circle inside it as the highlight. Add the nostril by making a small, dark circles roughly at the center of the face. Add an upward curving line for the mouth.

Figure 121. Add more fur to the limbs

12. Put more detail by making more feathered lines with your pencil throughout the chimp's body.

Figure 122. Begin shading the body

13. Once you have done so, you can begin shading the body starting with the underside by the belly and then the legs and arms.

Figure 123. Shade the face to bring out the features

14. Shading the face can be kind of tricky, but do not be confused. Start by shading delicately over where the brows should be and then give it cheekbones and a jaw by shading the side of the face. Be sure to shade around the mouth area as well so it has lips.

Figure 124. finalized drawing of the monkey

15. Put more shading to volumize the body of the monkey.

Chapter 15: How to Draw a Giraffe

The giraffe, like the zebra, is one of the zoo animals that have characteristics that make them easy to identify. They also have characteristics that are already quite familiar since they look similar to horses, ponies, and donkeys as well, but unlike the zebra, the giraffe has a lot of characteristics that differ remarkably from the horse, even if it has a lot of similarities.

Drawing materials used:

- 7B for outlining.
- 4B for shading.
- Eraser.

Tips and pointers

Before drawing the giraffe, let's analyze the differences and similarities to the horse and zebra. It is important to note that the neck length of the giraffe makes it very much unique from other animals. The length of its neck as well as the length of the legs makes it significantly taller than both the horse and zebra even if the legs are more or less shaped the same.

Unlike the horse, it's body slopes steeply from the neck to the rear. The giraffe also has a horn-like structure on its head. Its face, however is shaped similarly to the horse and the zebra, but the tail is more similar to the zebra than the horse. It also has markings like the zebra, but the pattern is different. As opposed to stripes, the zebra has patches of brown on its body. Keeping those characteristics in mind as we begin, it should be easier to draw the giraffe.

Step-by-step instructions on how to draw a giraffe

Figure 125. Begin with the general shapes

1. You can start drawing a giraffe by making two circles. One big circle (for the shoulder area) and then another that is smaller (for the rear) and then a triangle to represent the head.

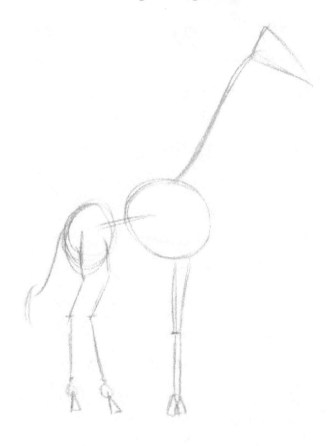

Figure 126. connect the neck and limbs by drawing lines

2. Next add small circles to represent the joints where the legs connect to the body. Add straight lines to represent the legs and put

small circle to represent the knees. Add small triangles to represent the hooves.

Figure 127. Draw the neck thickly and tapering towards the head

3. Now you can thicken-out the wireframes by connecting the shoulder part and the rear with two lines, and then joining the head with the shoulder by adding two lines again. After this, you should have something that looks like the neck and the body. The neck should be long and the body should taper towards the rear (while the neck tapers going up to the head.)

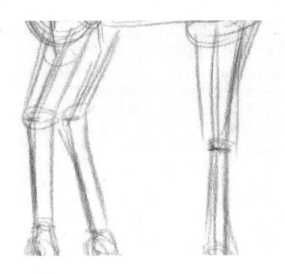

Figure 128. Thicken the limbs

4. Draw the legs thicker around the wireframe but still slender like this.

Figure 129. Add the outline for the tail

5. Add an outline of the hair and tail as well as the hooves, like in the above picture.

Figure 130. Outline without the wireframe

6. Erase any unneeded lines like those at the neck, at the middle parts of the body that connects to the legs and at the knees.

Figure 131. Cleaner outline of a giraffe

7. Smoothen out your lines. The giraffe doesn't have fur so, you can go on ahead and draw smooth, flowing lines when outlining the body.

Figure 132. Bring life into the eyes

8. After outlining the drawing, you can now detail it. You can begin detailing by adding the eyes. The eyes are drawn by making an arc and a crescent on top of each other and a circle inside it. Once you have made the circle, fill it out with dark shading, but leave a small circle inside it as the highlight. Add the nostril by making a dark circle near the end of the muzzle. It doesn't need to be a full circle just half will make it appear more real. Add a line for the mouth.

Figure 133. Add the pattern of the skin

9. This time we detail the whole body by adding its patches. The zebras stripes patches are bigger along the middle part and get smaller around the face-part, rear, and legs.

Figure 134. add the hair

10. Next, add some details to the hair by making short strokes for the hair such that it looks a bit like a brush and then draw the hair by the tail at the ends of it.

Figure 135. Make additional shading strokes

11. Add after that you can add the shading at the legs and the underside of the giraffe as well as the face. Darken the inner part of the patches.

Chapter 16: How to Draw an Eagle

Even though we have learned how to draw a bird before, learning to draw an eagle will be quite different. Smaller birds have a different shape than larger ones and the one we learned about before is roughly just a tenth of the size of an eagle so, there will be quite a lot of differences, from the shape of the beak to the wing span, and the length of the tail feather.

Drawing materials used:

- 7B for outlining.
- 4B for shading.
- Eraser.

Tips and pointers

As stated in the introduction, there will be a lot of differences when drawing the bird that we have learned to draw in the previous chapters and how to draw an eagle. First of all, the body shape is more elaborate than most smaller birds. The head shape won't be a simple rounded shape, the body will be longer and the torso more apparent, the tail is significantly longer just like the wing span and even the beak shape is different. The assortment of the different shapes and sizes of feathers will also be more apparent as we proceed with the lesson.

Step-by-step instructions on how to draw an eagle

Figure 136. The wireframe starts with two oval shapes

1. You can start drawing an eagle by drawing two circles. Draw one small circle for the head and then make one large oval for the body.

Figure 137. Begin to draw the outline for the wings

2. After that, draw the tail and then draw the wings twice the size of the oval that represents the body. Draw a curving cone for the beak. Make straight lines that fork into three lines at the end.

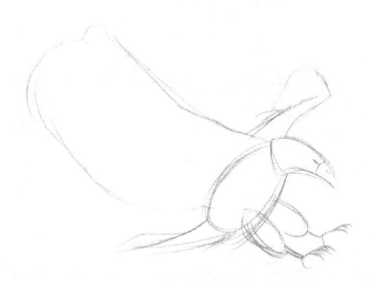

Figure 138. thicken out your wireframe

3. Next, draw a more detailed outline of the eagle by thickening out the legs into ovals. Thicken out the neck and connect it to the body.

Figure 139. Cleaner outline of the eagle

4. Erase any unneeded lines like those at the neck, at the middle parts of the body that connects to the legs and at the knees.

5. Detail the wings a bit more by drawing crescents to signify where the feathers will lie. At the outer part of the wings, draw lines representing the feathers tentatively. Plot where the eyes and the nostrils will lie, as well as where the beak will start.

Figure 140. Pay attention to how the feathers are illustrated

6. The next step is adding more details to the feathers. For the feathers of the body and the inner part of the wings, make lines that look like above.

Figure 141. The outer part of the wing's feathers are longer

7. For feathers at the outer part of the wings, draw longer feathers that spread outward.

Figure 142. notice the different 'feather sizes'

8. Draw the feathers at the tail and legs similarly. The feathers at the end of the tail should be long like in the out part of the wings.

Figure 143. Draw the claws

9. Thicken out the claws by drawing them like the above image.

Figure 144. Begin to add shading to the wings

10. Add after that you can add the shading at the legs and the underside of the eagle as well as the wings.

Figure 145. Draw the details of the face

11. Add the details of the face by making a slightly slanted line with three half crescents for the eyes and then darken the inner part. For the nose make a dot and then a curving line for the mouth.

Figure 146. Darken under the wings

12. Add more shading to give the drawing more depth.

Chapter 17: How to Draw a Deer

Drawing the deer is similar to drawing the horse in many ways. The body is shaped the same with differences in leg thickness, face shape (particularly at the nose area), and the tail. The deer also has antlers, as opposed to the horse which has none. Let's learn more in the tips section on how to draw the deer.

Drawing materials used:

- 7B for outlining.
- 4B for shading.
- Eraser.

Tips and pointers

As discussed in the introduction, drawing the horse and drawing a deer can be quite similar. I'm sure that the similarities in body shape are already obvious so, let's just discuss the differences instead. First and foremost, deer (the males) have antlers, which horses do not have. Second, the face shape is quite similar except that the deer has a pointier muzzle and a nose that looks more like the nose of a cow than the horse. Third, the horse has hair while the deer does not. Even the tail is different in that the tail of a deer is shorter and is not made of long strands of hair. And then finally, the deer has thinner legs than the horse. Try to remember these differences when drawing a deer. Let's begin:

Step-by-step instructions on how to a deer

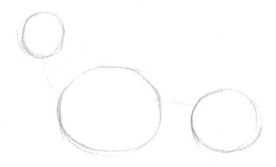

Figure 147. Start drawing the wireframe by drawing three circles

1. First, draw the wireframes by making three circles, one slightly larger than the other, and then one small one to represent the head.

Figure 148. Add the limbs, tail and horns

2. Connect the circles with lines then proceed to
   making the wireframe of the tail, the legs, the
   hooves, and the joints as with small circles and
   straight lines like above.

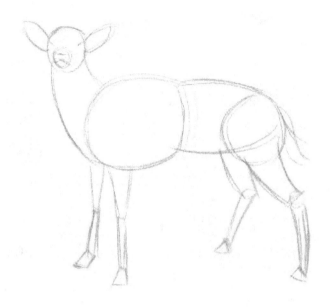

Figure 149. Thicken the wireframes

3. Next fill-out the wireframes by thickening the parts into general shapes using cylindrical or tube-like shapes. The legs should be thickened out into conical shapes that taper or become narrower as they reach the hooves. The neck should look like a thick cone connected to the head. Add some ears to the head.

Figure 150.Detail the wireframe for the antlers

4. Draw the wireframe for the antlers like above.
   Not all deer have antlers, particularly the
   females. The shape and size also vary, but this
   one will be our standard for this drawing.

Figure 151. Create a cleaner outline

5. After creating the wireframe for the antlers,
    you can begin to make a clean outline by
    erasing the extra lines when you made the
    wireframe particularly by the legs and neck and
    the middle of the body. Draw the outline using
    smoother and more curved lines. You can also
    now add a rough sketch of the tail.

Figure 152. Begin adding the details of the face

6. Now that you have an outline for the body, you can add the details of the face. You can start with the eyes by drawing a circle and then an arc over it. The nose can be drawn as a squarish shape that is rounded at the edges.

Figure 153. Begin shading the body

7. Now comes the shading. Try to shade in the right places by the legs and the shoulder area as well as the neck. Unlike the horse, shade the deer in a smoother way that doesn't define the muscles so much.

Figure 154. Define the body shape by darkly shading

8. When shading the deer's body, use broad and smooth pencil strokes when shading so it looks more realistic. Be sure to make the transition from heavier to light shading by shading smoothly.

Figure 155.Shade around the face

9. The same goes for shading the antlers. Keep
   the shading to one side so that it looks realistic.

Figure 156. Notice the tail and how it is drawn

10. Drawing the deer's tail is not like drawing the horse's tail which is composed more of hair. The deer's tail is shorter but more solid like in the picture.

Figure 157. Finalized drawing

11. Draw the outline darker and add more shading
    to bring out the shape of the body.

Chapter 18: How to Draw a Rabbit

You may have learned how to draw rabbits before or have been drawing rabbits before: Circle for a body, circle for the head, and two ears, at least that's how children commonly draw them. In this chapter, we will also begin drawing the rabbit this way, but we will be using a step-by-step process and get more into the details of how to draw a rabbit.

Drawing materials used:

- 7B for outlining.
- 4B for shading.
- Eraser.

Tips and pointers

The rabbit is closely related to rodents so, you might notice that it has several characteristics that it's 'cousins' possess. Some species of rabbits have a similar fur quality, like the hamster. The way the nose is shaped as well as the mouth and teeth also resemble the hamsters' and mice. The way the body is shaped— short forelegs and a bigger set of hind legs also run in the rodent family. Their eyes, however are bigger, the ears are significantly longer, and the tail is bushy rather than long. Let's learn more on how to draw rabbits as we begin the step-by-step instructions of how to draw rabbits.

Step-by-step instructions on how to draw a rabbit

Figure 158. Three circles for the head, body and torso

1. You can start drawing a rabbit by making three circles. One for the head, one for the body, and one for the rear. Make the circle for the head smaller than the other two. Make the one for the rear the biggest one.

Figure 159. Additional two circles for where the legs are situated

2. Draw more circles, one for the joints for the forelegs, and then a bigger one for the back legs.

Figure 160. Add the wireframe for the limbs

3. Next, draw lines to represent the legs, two straight lines at the front and then lines perpendicular to each other at the back.

Figure 161. Draw balls to represent the joints

4. Put circled half way through each of the legs to represent the joints.

Figure 162. Add the wireframe for the feet

168

5. Draw small triangular shapes for the feet of the forelegs.

Figure 163. Draw the wireframe of the face

6. Draw a cup-like shape for the snout and some arcs around the circle representing the face as the cheeks. Draw the eyes, the nose and mouth tentatively. The noses' general shape is an inverted triangle while the mouth is an inverted 'Y' shape. Add the ears tentatively by representing it with two leaf-shaped figures.

Figure 164. Bulk out the wireframe

7. You can now start thickening out the wireframe into more solid shapes. Connect the big circle together with two lines so that it becomes something like a thick, bent tube and then connect the shoulder to the head similarly. Thicken out the legs into tube-like shaped and thicken out the legs as well.

Figure 165. Erase the wireframe and other unnecessary lines

8. Finally, erase some of the unneeded lines
   around the body, particularly where the front
   part of the body is adjacent to the legs and the
   middle lines between the front and rear as well
   as by the neck and snout.

Figure 166. Begin drawing the fur-outline

9. After outlining the drawing, change the outline into feathered strokes that represent hair/fur. For a hairy, furry animal like the rabbit, it is better to outline it with pencil strokes that look like hair as opposed to a stiff flat line that will not convey the soft texture that the fur should possess. Add broad and smooth pencil strokes to add depth to the shape of the rabbit. Shade delicately around the underside part of the

rabbit and the legs. Shading at the middle will also help make it look fuller.

Figure 167. Drawing with added details

10. Add further details by making more feathered pencil strokes by the underside and the middle.

Figure 168. Shade the ears and add the whiskers

11. Add the whiskers by making long stokes
    outward with your pencil. Shade around the
    nose delicately then shade the ears to look
    hollow.

Figure 169. finalized drawing of a rabbit

12. Add more shading by darkening around the
    underside and the legs to make it pop out
    more.

Chapter 19: How to Draw a Tiger

In this chapter, we will be tackling the topic of how to draw a tiger. Once you have learned how to draw a cat and a lion, drawing the tiger will become easier as they share a similar wireframe. The tiger, like the lion is only bigger in size and has distinct markings so you will have to adjust accordingly. Continue reading below for the details of how to draw a tiger.

Drawing materials used:

- 7B for outlining.
- 4B for shading.
- Eraser.

Tips and pointers

The tiger is a fierce, yet graceful creature so, this must be communicated in your drawing when drawing a tiger. In learning how to draw a lion and a cat, it is important to pay close attention on how the head is shaped, the texture of the fur, and the way the body is drawn. The same goes for drawing a tiger. Not unlike the lion, its face is bigger and longer than a house cat's. Unlike the lion, however, the tiger doesn't have hair or thick fur on its head so, the head looks more balanced with the rest of the body. You will also need to pay close attention to drawing the markings or the stripes on its body as this is easily the most distinct feature of the tiger. Let's begin.

Step-by-step instructions on how to draw a tiger

Figure 170. wireframe of a tiger

1. Let's begin by drawing the wireframe of the tiger using a medium sized circle for the head, a big circle for the shoulder to torso area, and then another medium sized circle for the rear. At this point you can have small circles to represent the part where the shoulder and leg joints are.

Figure 171. Add the muzzle and tentative details for the face

2. Add the muzzle to the circle (representing the head by drawing a cylinder). The wireframe should look something like the cats', only bigger. Try not to make the wireframe look stiff as following a stiff wireframe can result in a stiff looking drawing. Use flowing, fluid pencil strokes.

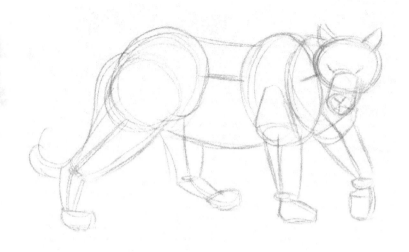

Figure 172. thicken out the wireframe

3. After finishing the wireframe, you can now bulk-up your drawing using the general shapes we have been using in the previous chapters. Cylinders are great for fleshing out the legs and circles are a great way to pinpoint where the joints bend. Connect the shoulder area with the rear area such that it tapers toward the rear. Draw the neck thickly. Compared to the bear, the muzzle of the tiger is shorter and wider so, draw it like above.

Figure 173. Erase the wireframe

4. At this point you can start erasing the unneeded lines starting with the wireframe and refining the outline.

Figure 174. Add the details of the tiger's face

5. Add the details of the face by drawing the ears, the eyes, and the nose. Put dots just below the nose, and add whiskers by drawing with thin lines.

Figure 175. You can now begin shading the body

6. Shade the body of the tiger by making broad smooth strokes. The tiger has very short fur around the body so, there is not much need to detail strokes of it. Broad strokes of shading will do.

Figure 176. Add some shading to the face

7. Bring some depth to the face by the making light shading around it.

Figure 177. Begin to draw the stripes

8. Now, you can draw the markings on the body. Make broad stripe marks on the center of the body and make them thinner as they reach the ends of the body as well as the legs and face.

Figure 178. Finalized drawing of a tiger

9. Add some more shading so that the shape of the body has more depth. Shade darkly around the edges so that the center looks highlighted.

Chapter 20: How to Draw a Snake

In this chapter, we will be tackling the topic of how to draw a snake. There are a lot of species of snakes and there's a different way of drawing each of them, but for now we will learn how to draw a garden snake. The snake is unlike any other animal that we have tackled in the discussions so far. The snake has no legs nor arms or fur, and the lack of limbs makes it easier to draw. However, in drawing snakes, the attention devoted to making the arms and legs has to be given to illustrating the texture of its skin so be sure to observe and practice what you will learn in the step-by-step instructions of how to draw a snake.

Drawing materials used:

- 7B for outlining.
- 4B for shading.
- Eraser.

Tips and pointers

In drawing the snake, it is useful to imagine a fat rope or a coiling tube as this is the general shape of a snake. As stated earlier, one has to pay close attention to how the skin of the snake is drawn as this is one of the most unique characteristics of the snake, aside from the lack of limbs and fur. Make sure to bring out the glossiness and the shine in the skin as well as the scaly texture of it.

Step-by-step instructions on how to draw a snake

Figure 179. The wireframe should look like a coil

1. Creating the wire-frame for the snake is fairly easy. You just have to draw a flat spiral and then draw a triangle-like shape for the head at the end of it.

Figure 180. Thicken out the wireframe

2. At this point, you can already thicken out by creating lines parallel lines on both sides of the wireframe that you made so that you can slowly start to thicken out the snake's body. Again, it helps to imagine a coiled tube while drawing.

Figure 181. Add more bulk to the head

3. Next, erase the wireframe and then thicken out the triangle shape you made for the head of the snake. Soften out the edges so it doesn't look too pointy.

Figure 182. Begin shading the body

4. Next, shade the body of the snake by creating smooth pencil strokes by the underside of the snake's body and just a little bit at the top by the head and at the ends. Make sure that the shading on the underside is darker.

Figure 183. add stopples to bring out the texture

5. Add more details by making stippled pencil strokes to illustrate the scaliness of the skin.

Figure 184. Make the eyes look beady

6. Add more details by drawing the elements of the face. A snake has a bead-like eye so, draw a circle and then darken around the center,

leaving a small ring and small circle as the highlights.

Figure 185. Finalized drawing of a snake

7. Add more shading, darkening the underside parts better.

Chapter 21: How to Draw a Turtle

In this chapter, we will be tackling the topic of how to draw a turtle. There are different types of turtles. There are sea turtles, tortoises, etc. --and there are different ways of drawing each of them, but for now we will learn how to draw a box turtle, which is more common as a house pet and is of a smaller variety compared to other types of turtles. Most likely you have already seen a turtle, whether in real life or in pictures. I'm sure you will agree that the most characteristic feature of this animal is its shell so pay close attention in observing how the turtle's shell looks like before drawing.

Drawing materials used:

- 7B for outlining.
- 4B for shading.
- Eraser.

Tips and pointers

In drawing the turtle, as stated earlier, one must pay close attention to drawing the shell since this is the most important part of the turtle. Also, make sure to study how the skin is drawn carefully. The turtle's skin is a combination of many textures but primarily, the box turtle's skin is rather rough and the skin by the neck is thin and a bit loose so, you'd need to study pictures of turtles carefully to see which part tends to have what kind of texture. The same goes for the shell of the turtle. It is not a simple smooth shell, but one that has bumps and curves. Be sure that those textures show up in your drawing.

Step-by-step instructions on how to draw a turtle

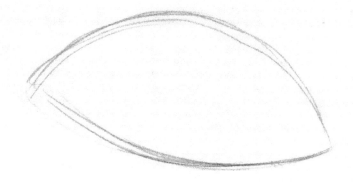

Figure 186. Draw the basic shape for the shell

1. Creating the wire-frame for the turtle is quite easy. Just begin by drawing an arch and then a line below it to close it off.

Figure 187. Draw the wireframe for the underside of the shell

2. Add a boat like shape below. The turtle's soft body is encased in the shell so we have to draw two 'parts' of a shell that encloses the entire body. It should look kind of like a lopsided hamburger after.

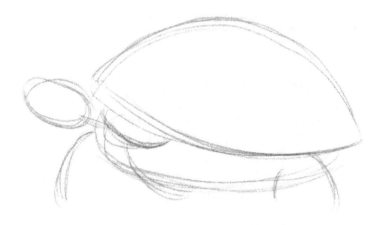

Figure 188. add general shapes for the head and limbs

3. Next, add lines for the neck and legs, and then a circle for the head and lines for the legs.

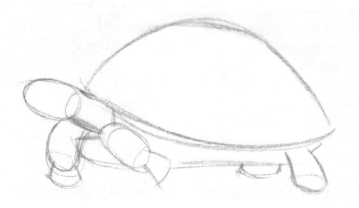

Figure 189. thicken out the wireframe

4. Once you have created the wireframe, it's time to thicken the drawing out. Start with thickening out the legs into tube-like shapes. The turtles' leg is stumpy, so the 'feet' look like they are directly a part of the leg. Do the same with the neck and connect it to the head and the body.

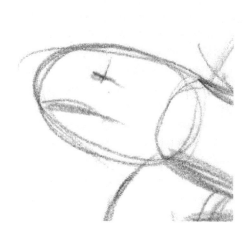

Figure 190. Plot out where the details of the face will lie

5. Add 'markers' for where the face elements (eyes, nose, and mouth) should lie.

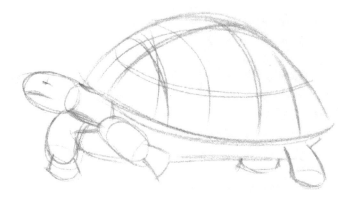

Figure 191. Draw a grid on it's back

6. Draw grid-like lines across the back of the turtle on the shell. This will serve as a guide on how to shade the turtle's back and give it texture and shape later.

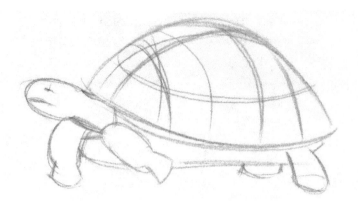

Figure 192. Erase unnecessary lines

7. Erase the wireframe lines by the head and the neck and smoothen out your outline.

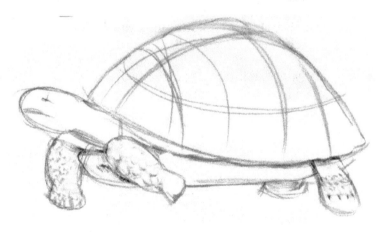

Figure 193. Start bringing out the texture of the skin

8. Next, add more details by making stippled pencil strokes to illustrate the scaliness and bumpiness of the skin by the legs. Use the blunt end of your pencil to do this. Add some shading to the legs and the underside of the turtle. Use

smoother strokes for the underside of the turtle's body as well as when shading the sides of the legs.

Figure 194. Pay close attention to the pattern on the turtle's back

9. Draw these kinds of patterns on the turtle's shell by using the blunt end of your pencil.

Figure 195. Add the details of the face

10. Add more details by drawing the elements of the face. Draw a circle and then darken around the center, leaving a small circle as the highlight, and then draw an arc around it. After that, draw some rings around the eyes of the turtle like this.

Figure 196. Start shading the face

11. As described earlier, the neck of the turtle is rather loose so, be sure to shade it so that the highlights look like 'lines' and the deeper parts of the skin should be darkly, but smoothly shaded.

Figure 197. Finalized drawing of a turtle

12. Be sure to also shade around the face so that
the roundedness around the cheeks are
apparent.

Chapter 22: How to Draw a Mouse

The mouse is one of the animals that is very easy to picture when it is mentioned. It is small, has beady eyes and small limbs, a roundish or oval-shaped body, and then a tail. That being said, it won't be too hard to draw the mouse once you learn how to illustrate specific parts of this animal. One important thing to focus on is the overall shape of the mouse. In this chapter, we will learn how to draw a field mouse which is one variety of mouse that is great to start practicing drawings with. Read on to learn more about how to draw a mouse.

Drawing materials used:

- 7B for outlining.
- 4B for shading.
- Eraser.

Tips and pointers

Learning how the hamster is drawn will help you learn how to draw a mouse. The hamster and the mouse have similar facial features, only the mouse is less hairy than the hamster. The roundish shape of the body is more obvious because of this. The ears are also larger and the tail is longer. Let's proceed learning how to draw the mouse with the help of the step by step procedure below.

Step-by-step instructions on how to draw a mouse

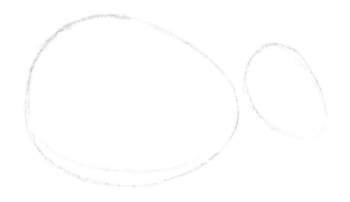

Figure 198. Start with two egg-like shapes

1. You can start drawing a mouse by making two egg-like shapes like above.

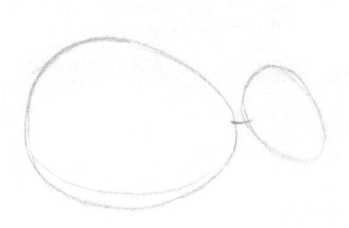

2. Those two shapes will represent the head and the body. As you see in the example, one egg-like shape is bigger than the other so, make sure to follow that. Next, connect the head and the body with a line.

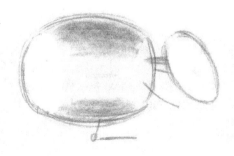

Figure 199. Add the limbs and connect the head to the body

3. Draw two circles to represent the upper part of the hind legs, then draw two lines perpendicular to each other to represent the legs themselves, and then lines sticking out of the front part of the body for the arms.

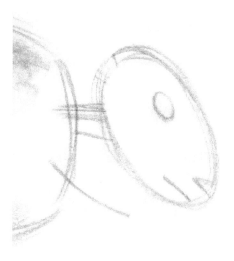

Figure 200. Plot where the details of the face will lie

4. Draw the eyes, the nose, and mouth tentatively. The noses' general shape is a 'V' shape attached to the end of the face because the mouse is in profile-view. Draw a line for the mouth.

Figure 201. Add the tail and the hands and feet

5. Draw small triangular shapes for the feet and then skewed circles with lines as the hands.

Figure 202. Add the ears

6. Add the ears by creating oval shapes on top of the head.

Figure 203. Create a cleaner outline

7. At this point, you can start thickening the legs and arms as well as the neck by joining the neck to the body and then erase some of the unneeded lines around the body (particularly by the hind legs), by the arms, and the neck.

Figure 204. Start outlining with fur

8. At this point, you can start outlining the body of the mouse. Like the hamster, the outline shouldn't be a smooth continuous line. We need to show the texture of the hamster's hair so, we will have to outline the hair with short strokes of the pencil because the mouse has short hair.

Figure 205. Draw the eyes

9. Add more realism by drawing the eye, nose, and mouth with more detail. The eyes should be big, beady, and shiny so, darken the circle and leave a spot of white at the edge for the highlight.

Figure 206. Add more strokes to the body to create a fur-like texture

10. Create more details by putting more short strokes of the pencil around the mouse's body so that it looks like it has fur all over. Avoid putting strokes of hair for the legs and hands, those should be outlined smoothly.

Figure 207. Begin detailing the face

11. Shade around the nose delicately then shade the ears to look hollow and wrinkled near the head and by its edges. Be sure to add hair around the face as well and don't forget to add dots below the nose as well as whiskers. Make the whiskers by making long stokes outward with your pencil.

Figure 208. finalized drawing of a mouse with shading

12. Add broad and smooth pencil strokes to add
    depth to the shape of the hamster. Shade
    delicately around the underside part of the
    mouse, as well as the legs and arms. Shading at
    the middle will also help make it look fuller.

Chapter 23: How to Draw a Wolf

In this chapter, we are going to learn how to draw wolves, which is similar to drawing dogs. We need to note, however, that there are notable differences between the two. Once you learn the differences, you must remember them and make note of them as you begin drawing a wolf.

Drawing materials used:

- 7B for outlining.
- 4B for shading.
- Eraser.

Tips and pointers

In learning how to draw a dog, it is important to pay close attention on how the head is shaped, the fur quality, and the way the legs are drawn. The same can be said about drawing wolves. However, we need to note that wolves usually hang their head lower than dogs so that the posture is quite different. Also, the wolves' fur is usually thick and shaggy to protect it from the cold. Some dog breeds. however, also have thick fur, and Alaskan malamutes and huskies especially resemble wolves for that reason. It is also useful to not that, unlike the dog that usually has a warm and friendly look on its face (given it's not angry of course), the wolf looks more intimidating and fierce because of the almond shaped eyes and the markings around them so, try to bring all of these elements into your drawing when drawing a wolf.

Step-by-step instructions on how to draw a wolf

Figure 209. Begin drawing the wireframe for the wolf

1. As with drawing a dog, drawing a wolf also begins with making the wireframe. Start by drawing three circles. The one for the shoulder/torso should be the biggest and the one for the rear should be smaller. The smallest should be for the head and make this one more oval shaped. Connect the circles with lines connecting them.

Figure 210. A more detailed wireframe

2. Next, create lines for the legs and arms and put circles where the joints and paws should be like above. Add the snout and the ears. The snout should be a cone-like shape and the ears should be triangles on top of the head.

Figure 211. Begin thickening the wireframe

3. Now that you have a guide for estimating where the features will lie, you can start adding them by filling up the wire-frame with basic shapes of circles and cylinders. The joints of the limbs are represented by small circles. The torso area of the wolf is bigger than the rear end of it, as you can see in this example so, try to pattern your drawing after that.

Figure 212. Erase the unnecessary lines

4. At this point you'll be able to outline the body of the wolf. It is easier to start with the main outline first before adding in the details. Feel free to erase the wireframe and the bulked wire-frame guide so that you have a cleaner looking drawing.

Figure 213. A more detailed outline

5. Like in drawing the dog, it is better to draw the fur as the outline itself rather than drawing a flat continuous line. The fur should be illustrated in feathered strokes, like so.

Figure 214. Draw the eyes

6. Now that you have an outline for the body, you can add the details starting with the face. You

can start with the eyes. Drawing the wolf's eyes in a way that it conveys fierceness is important as this is one of its prominent features. The eyes should be slanting up at the outer edge and slanting down at the inner edge.

Figure 215. Add the mouth

7. The wolf's nose is kind of a 'U' shape so, draw it like the letter u with the nostrils. Draw the mouth by making two lines starting from the base of the nose outward and a bit turned down at the ends. In this drawing, the wolf's mouth is open and the tongue hangs out—something that the wolf commonly does so, we're going to draw the mouth like this in this guide. Add dots around the nose and add the whiskers by

drawing thin lines outwards. Make sure the lines are not heavy and it should taper from heavy to thin, like so.

Figure 216. Shade the face

8. Make some shading to bring out the solidity of the dog's face. Shade delicately and shade by using these kinds of pencil strokes. These kinds of strokes can be achieved by tilting your pencil and using the flatter end so that the shading comes out broad, but smooth.

Figure 217.Start shading the body

9. Add more volume by adding additional details of fur on the body, but putting more feathered strokes like in making the outline of its body.

Figure 218. Finalized drawing of a wolf

10. Darken the shading and the outline to bring out the fullness of the wolf's body.

Chapter 24: How to Draw a Lizard

In this chapter, we will be discussing the how to draw a lizard. Like the other animals that have been tackled, there are a lot of different species of lizards and there's a different way of drawing each of them, but for now we will focus on how to draw a certain type of lizard. In drawing a lizard, it is important to pay attention on how to bring out the texture of its scaly and bumpy skin.

Drawing materials used:

- 7B for outlining.
- 4B for shading.
- Eraser.

Tips and pointers

In drawing a lizard, it is useful to look up close-up pictures of the animal first so that you have an idea of the texture you have to illustrate. Knowing how to draw its skin is one of the most important parts of drawing a lizard. Even if you don't get it the first time, it's okay, just be sure to observe and practice more.

Step-by-step instructions on how to draw a lizard

1. Creating the wire-frame for the lizard starts with drawing an oval for a head and then a long straight line for the body and tail.

Figure 219. Wireframe of a lizard

2. Next, add the arms by making four lines (to represent the limbs) attached to the straight line that represents the body. Make sure around half of it is left for the tail.

Figure 220. Wireframe with the face and hands

3. Next, add the parts of the face tentatively along with triangles with lines sticking out of them to represent the fingers.

Figure 221. thicken the wireframe

4. After the wireframe and face has been made, thicken out the body of the lizard by drawing lines parallel to the wireframe lines you have created.

Figure 222. Outline of the lizard

5. You can now erase the wireframe at this point and any other unneeded lines.

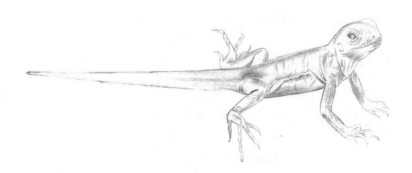

Figure 223. Outline with added shading

6. Start adding more details by adding texture to the skin by making lines across the skin that looks like wrinkles. This can be added by shading the skin. Make the shading smooth by using the flat part of your pencil.

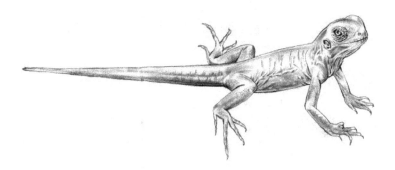

Figure 224. Finalized drawing

7. Darken the shading and the outline more to bring out the shape of the lizard's body.

Conclusion

Thank you for taking the time to read this e-book on *How to Draw Animals*. I hope that this e-book has been able to help you learn how to draw animals with the step-by-step procedure used and I hope that you had enjoyed learning.

Now that you have the fundamental knowledge on how to draw animals, I hope that you will not stop practicing and learning. Practicing regularly will help you draw better and faster, as well as achieve a drawing that is more life-like and natural. One good way of keeping up with your practice is to study pictures and videos of animals and drawing various kinds of animals and their poses from this material.

Even if the progress of learning to draw of achieving a good drawing might be slow, I hope that you will not get discouraged. This should only encourage you to practice more so that you will get better and better with time. Looking at beautifully done sketches of animals is a great way to encourage yourself to work harder and should bring some inspiration when you feel like giving up. Communicating with other artists, or seeking advice from them on forums or communities like http://www.deviantart.com will not only help you improve on drawing animals, but should also motivate you to draw more and draw better. You might encounter criticism from time to time and I advise not to take them personally, but try to learn from them.

About the Expert

Therese Barleta has been drawing for over 20 years. Ever since the time she can hold a pencil, she has been drawing and has been improving this skill in realistic drawing continuously. Growing up, art has always been her passion and while still studying in grade school, she always dreamed of pursuing a career in the arts. While in school, she accepted arts commissions and eventually ended up with landing an illustrator position for a storyboard company as her first job. The company she worked for has given illustrating services for U.S and U.K. based companies, such as Wendy's, Ford Motors, and Yoplait to name a few.

During Therese Barleta's childhood years, her mother always gave her a pencil and a stack of papers to draw on, which she would doodle various images on. As the doodles developed into recognizable drawings of animals and people, her family discovered that she had a knack for drawing and they encouraged her to keep practicing this skill. Comic books, such as Archie, Marvel, and, eventually, Manga, nurtured her love for drawing and then later developed her skill for drawing realistically when Interactive Arts Services employed her as a storyboard penciller. The job required constant drawing of different people of different ages, sexes, and races depicting various everyday situations and this constant practice sharpened her skill in realistic drawing.

For budding artists, Therese Barleta advises: *"Learn to appreciate and enjoy drawing first as a passion, something that you really love to do and not something that you need to do. Looking at other people's beautiful works will help inspire you and fire-up your interests. The inspiration will give you the desire to grab a pencil and paper and start drawing. Never lose heart and just keep on practicing and be sure to always enjoy what you're doing. When looking at great artists' works, don't just look, appreciate and absorb how the person executes their drawing. Look, appreciate and learn."*

HowExpert publishes quick 'how to' guides on all topics from A to Z by everyday experts. Visit HowExpert.com to learn more.

Recommended Resources

- HowExpert.com – Quick 'How To' Guides on All Topics from A to Z by Everyday Experts.
- HowExpert.com/free – Free HowExpert Email Newsletter.
- HowExpert.com/books – HowExpert Books
- HowExpert.com/courses – HowExpert Courses
- HowExpert.com/clothing – HowExpert Clothing
- HowExpert.com/membership – HowExpert Membership Site
- HowExpert.com/affiliates – HowExpert Affiliate Program
- HowExpert.com/jobs – HowExpert Jobs
- HowExpert.com/writers – Write About Your #1 Passion/Knowledge/Expertise & Become a HowExpert Author.
- HowExpert.com/resources – Additional HowExpert Recommended Resources
- YouTube.com/HowExpert – Subscribe to HowExpert YouTube.
- Instagram.com/HowExpert – Follow HowExpert on Instagram.
- Facebook.com/HowExpert – Follow HowExpert on Facebook.
- TikTok.com/@HowExpert – Follow HowExpert on TikTok.

CPSIA information can be obtained
at www.ICGtesting.com
Printed in the USA
BVHW032127141221
624086BV00001B/26